chewing the cud

For Petra

Thanks to Renée Lang, whose idea it was to create this book

First published in 2004 by New Holland Publishers (NZ) Ltd
Auckland • Sydney • London • Cape Town

218 Lake Road, Northcote, Auckland, New Zealand
14 Aquatic Drive, Frenchs Forest, NSW 2086, Australia
86–88 Edgware Road, London W2 2EA, United Kingdom
80 McKenzie Street, Cape Town 8001, South Africa

www.newhollandpublishers.co.nz

Copyright © 2004 in photography: Don Donovan
Copyright © 2004 New Holland Publishers (NZ) Ltd

ISBN: 1 86966 068 4

Publishing manager: Renée Lang
Project editor: Fionna Campbell
Design: Trevor Newman

A catalogue record for this book is available from the National
Library of New Zealand

10 9 8 7 6 5 4 3 2 1

Colour reproduction by SC (Sang Choy) International Pte Ltd,
Singapore
Printed in China through Phoenix Offset, Hong Kong

chewing the cud

DON DONOVAN

NEW
HOLLAND

Blessed are they who expect nothing for they shall not be disappointed!

ANONYMOUS

The important thing is not to stop questioning. Curiosity has its own reason for existing.

ALBERT EINSTEIN

**Laughing stock:
cattle with a sense
of humour.**

ANONYMOUS

We are all either fools or

undiscovered geniuses.   BONNIE LIN

See what will happen if you don't stop biting your fingernails?

WILL ROGERS

There are known knowns.
These are things we
know that we know.
There are known unknowns.
That is to say, there are things
we know we don't know.
But, there are also unknown
unknowns. These are things we
don't know we don't know.

DONALD RUMSFELD

All animals are created equal, but some are more equal than others.

GEORGE ORWELL

Anything worth doing is worth doing slowly.

MAE WEST

I don't believe
in reincarnation,
and I didn't believe
in it when I was a
hamster.

SHANE RITCHIE

**Get away from the crowd
when you can.
Keep yourself to yourself,
if only for a few hours daily.**

ARTHUR BRISBANE

A narcissist is someone better looking than you are.

GORE VIDAL

I tried marijuana once.
I did not inhale.

WILLIAM J. CLINTON

If I were two-faced, would I be wearing this one?

ABRAHAM LINCOLN

I have opinions of my own;
strong opinions; but I don't
always agree with them.

GEORGE BUSH SNR

Beautiful young people are accidents of nature, but beautiful old people are works of art.

ELEANOR ROOSEVELT

Everything comes

if a man will only wait. BENJAMIN DISRAELI

It's not the bulls and bears you need to avoid – it's the bum steers.

CHUCK HILLISS

Scientists tell us that the fastest animal on earth, with a top speed of 120 ft/sec, is a cow that has been dropped out of a helicopter.

DAVE BARRY

A good rest is half the work.

YUGOSLAV PROVERB

I am nobody. Nobody is perfect. Therefore, I must be perfect!

ANONYMOUS

Good cowgirls
keep their calves together.

OFF A WALL

**Three little maids
from school are we,
Pert as a school-girl
well can be,
Filled to the brim
with girlish glee,
Three little maids
from school!**

W.S. GILBERT

A gold rush is what happens when a line of chorus girls spots a man with a bank roll.

MAE WEST

**People who need people
are the luckiest people in
the world.**

BOB MERRILL

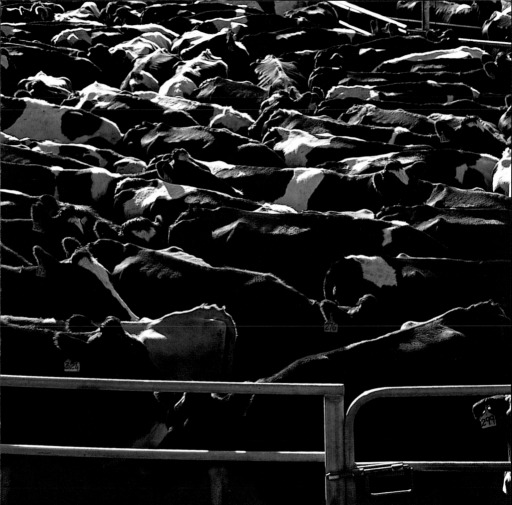

I awoke one morning and found myself famous.

LORD BYRON

We've got to pause and ask ourselves:

how much clean air do we need? LEE IACOCCA

Insanity is hereditary – you get it from your children

ANONYMOUS

Have you noticed that all the people in favour of birth control are already born?

BENNY HILL

Who discovered we could get milk from cows; and what did he think he was doing at the time?

BILLY CONNOLLY

... facts are like cows. If you look them in the face hard enough they generally run away.

DOROTHY L. SAYERS

I've developed a new philosophy –
I only dread one day at a time.

CHARLES M. SCHULZ

Don't threaten me with love, Baby.

Let's just go walking in the rain. BILLIE HOLIDAY

When choosing between two evils, I always like to try the one I've never tried before.

MAE WEST

Remember, if you smoke after sex you're doing it too fast.

WOODY ALLEN

You know your children are growing up when they stop asking you where they came from and refuse to tell you where they're going.

P. J. O'ROURKE

I am not a vegetarian because
I love animals; I am a vegetarian
because I hate plants.

A. WHITNEY BROWN

Some days you're the dog and some days you're the lamp post.

ANONYMOUS

My great-grandmother had an affair with your great grandfather.

CAMILLA PARKER BOWLES TO PRINCE CHARLES